W9-AYS-181

Saltwater Crocodile

by Tom Jackson

Consultants:

John E. McCosker, PhD
Chair of Aquatic Biology, California Academy of Sciences

Maureen Flannery, MS
Ornithology and Mammalogy Collection Manager, California Academy of Sciences

Wallace J. Nichols, PhD
Research Associate, California Academy of Sciences

BEARPORT
PUBLISHING

New York, New York

Publisher: Kenn Goin
Editorial Director: Adam Siegel
Creative Director: Spencer Brinker
Photo Researcher: Brown Bear Books Ltd

Library of Congress Cataloging-in-Publication Data

Jackson, Tom, 1972–
  Saltwater crocodile / by Tom Jackson.
     p. cm. — (The deep end: animal life underwater)
  Includes bibliographical references and index.
  ISBN-13: 978-1-61772-923-2 (library binding)
  ISBN-10: 1-61772-923-X (library binding)
  1. Crocodylus porosus—Juvenile literature. 2. Crocodiles—Juvenile literature. I. Title.
  QL666.C925J334 2014
  597.98'2—dc23
                    2013011638

For more information, write to Bearport Publishing Company, Inc., 45 West 21st Street, Suite 3B, New York, New York 10010. Printed in the United States of America.

10 9 8 7 6 5 4 3 2 1

Contents

Secret Swimmer

A wide river flows slowly through a steamy jungle.

Everything seems peaceful—until ripples begin to move out across the water.

Soon, two eyes start to rise from below the surface.

Then, a large head appears.

It belongs to a huge saltwater crocodile on the lookout for lunch!

nostril

eye

Most of the time, a saltwater crocodile stays hidden. It floats with just its eyes and **nostrils** above the surface of the water.

Ruling Reptile

The saltwater crocodile is the largest kind of crocodile in the world.

It's also the largest **reptile** in the world.

It's bigger than any snake, turtle, or lizard.

The biggest saltwater crocodiles are 23 feet (7 m) long.

That's more than half the length of a school bus.

There are 23 species, or kinds, of **crocodilians** in the world. This group includes crocodiles and closely related animals such as alligators.

Watery Homes

Saltwater crocodiles live in parts of Asia and Australia.

Like other kinds of crocodiles, they make their homes in **freshwater** rivers and swamps.

Unlike most other crocodiles, however, they also spend time in oceans.

These places are filled with saltwater.

As a result, the giant reptile was named the saltwater crocodile.

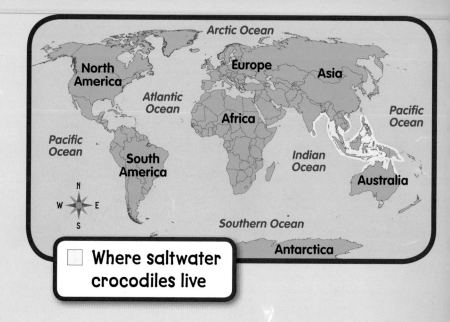

Arctic Ocean

North America

Europe

Asia

Atlantic Ocean

Africa

Pacific Ocean

Pacific Ocean

South America

Indian Ocean

Australia

N W E S

Southern Ocean

Antarctica

☐ Where saltwater crocodiles live

What do you think saltwater crocodiles eat?

In Australia, people often call saltwater crocodiles "salties" for short.

Hunting for Food

Saltwater crocodiles are excellent swimmers.

Yet they usually stay close to the water's edge.

Here, they can dive down to hunt for fish and crabs.

They can also float with just their eyes and nostrils showing.

This way, they can watch for food along the **coast** without being seen.

In Australia, saltwater crocodiles eat fish as well as animals that stop by a river for a drink, such as kangaroos, wild boars, or water buffalo.

Saltwater Crocodile Food

wild boar

water buffalo

kangaroo

river turtle

egret

How does a crocodile catch a large animal?

Grabbing a Meal

Saltwater crocodiles silently watch for animals that come close to the water's edge.

When an animal is near, a crocodile charges out of the water.

It snaps its jaws shut and grabs its **prey**.

Then it drags the animal into the water and drowns it.

prey

Although saltwater crocodiles have large teeth, they can't chew their food. They have to swallow fish whole and twist chunks of meat off larger animals.

fish

Danger! Crocs!

Saltwater crocodiles are very dangerous.

A big crocodile can kill an animal as big as a horse.

If a person gets too close, a crocodile will attack.

As a result, people in some places are taking action.

If saltwater crocodiles are nearby, they capture them and move them far away.

Every year, between 20 and 30 people are attacked by saltwater crocodiles. Most survive, but some are killed by the powerful animals.

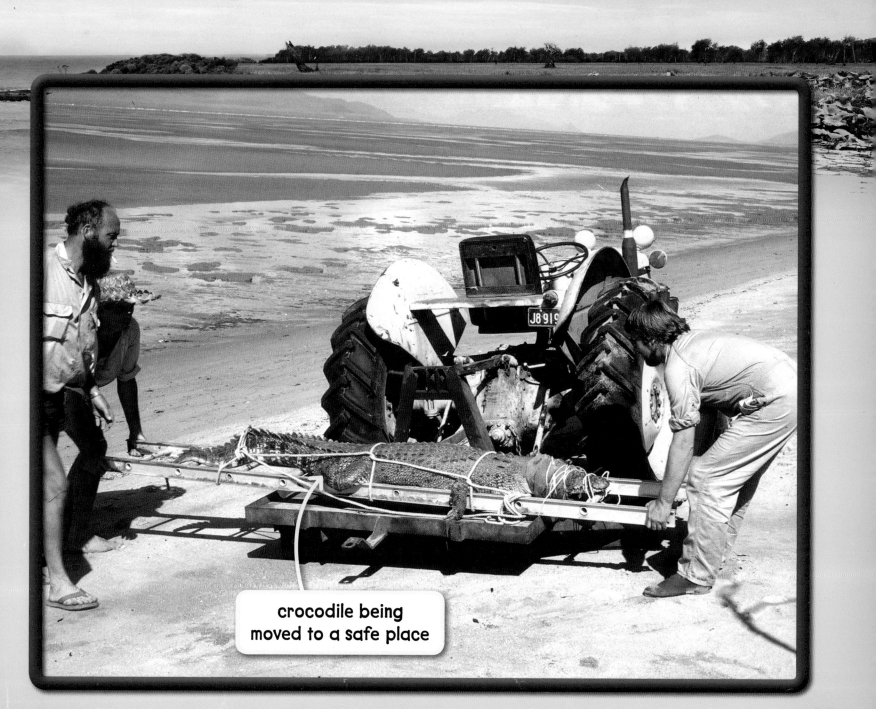

crocodile being
moved to a safe place

Making a Nest

Like all crocodiles, saltwater crocodiles hatch from eggs.

A female saltie lays 40 to 60 eggs on land, close to shore.

Then she buries them in a nest made from mud and leaves.

nest

eggs

mother

nest

A mother crocodile stays by her nest to defend it from large lizards, wild boars, and other egg-eating animals.

Do you think a mother crocodile cares for her babies once they hatch?

Baby Crocodiles

After about 80 days in the nest, the baby crocodiles hatch.

They squeak to tell their mother to come and dig them out.

After that, the babies don't stay on land for long.

The mother crocodile gently carries them to the water in her huge mouth.

She stays nearby as they learn to swim.

egg

baby crocodile

Surviving Danger

Life is dangerous for young crocodiles.

Fish, birds, and other animals catch and eat them.

Even older crocodiles will attack them.

Only a few saltwater crocodiles will live long enough to become adults.

If they survive that long, however, no other animal will dare to bother them.

They will rule the water as they swim in rivers, swamps, and out to sea.

crocklet

Saltwater crocodiles that survive to become adults may live for 70 years or more.

What Kind of Covering?

Many kinds of animals besides crocodiles live in the water. The different animals have different kinds of coverings on their bodies to help them survive. Some coverings help animals fly while others protect their bodies.

Can you match each covering to the animal it belongs to?

(The answers are on page 24.)

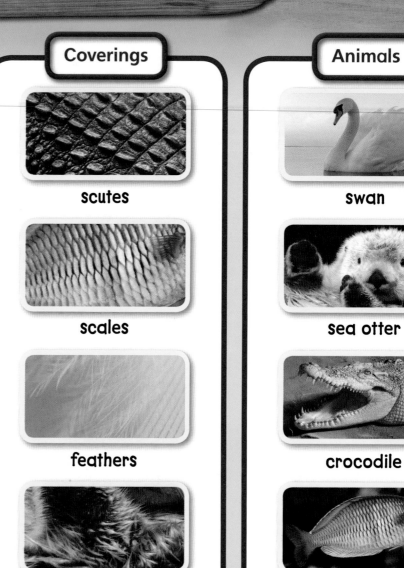

Coverings

scutes

scales

feathers

fur

Animals

swan

sea otter

crocodile

fish

Science Words

coast (KOHST)
land that runs along
an ocean

crocodilians
(krok-uh-DIL-yuhnz)
a group of animals made
up of crocodiles and their
close relations

freshwater (FRESH-*wa*-tur)
water that does not
contain salt

nostrils (NOSS-truhlz)
two openings in a
nose that are used for
breathing and smelling

prey (PRAY) an animal
that is hunted and eaten
by another animal

reptile (REP-tile)
a cold-blooded animal
that usually has dry,
scaly skin

Index

Read More

Kaufman, Gabriel. *Saltwater Crocodile: The World's Biggest Reptile (SuperSized!).* New York: Bearport (2007).

Marsico, Katie. *Saltwater Crocodiles (Nature's Children).* New York: Children's Press (2013).

Sexton, Colleen A. *The Saltwater Crocodile (Nature's Deadliest).* Minneapolis, MN: Bellwether Media (2012).

Learn More Online

To learn more about saltwater crocodiles, visit **www.bearportpublishing.com/TheDeepEnd**

Answers for Page 22

- Scutes cover crocodiles • Scales cover fish
- Feathers cover swans • Fur covers sea otters

About the Author

Tom Jackson learned about animals in college and has worked in zoos, African safari parks, and rain forests. He now writes books about natural history and science in his attic in England.